SEEING BEYOND AND EXPLORING COSMOS

A JOURNEY THROUGH THE WORLD OF TELESCOPES

KANCHANA MUNIRATHNAM

Dedicated to beloved universe

Contents

Foreword

Telescopes are in some ways like time machines. They reveal galaxies so far away that their light has taken billions of years to reach us. We in astronomy have an advantage in studying the universe because we can actually see the past."
- Carl Sagan

Preface

Our knowledge of Earth's position in the universe has advanced significantly since the invention of the telescope.The telescope is the most significant research instrument in astronomy. It offers a way to gather and examine details of celestial objects, even those located far out in space.

Telescope was a device for observing far-off objects that used lenses, curved mirrors, or a combination of the two. Telescope is now an instrument which has broad range of devices that can detect various electromagnetic spectrum regions in the universe.

Telescopes in space, such as the Hubble Space Telescope and the James Webb Space Telescope, have provided unprecedented views of the cosmos free from atmospheric interference. These space-based observatories have made groundbreaking discoveries, captured stunning images, and transformed our understanding of the universe.

Telescope ,a crucial scientific tool has altered our understanding of the cosmos.Overall, telescopes are indispensable tools for exploring, understanding, and appreciating the vastness and complexity of the universe.

CHAPTER ONE

INTRODUCTION

HISTORY

The history of telescopes as we know them today dates back many thousand years.The history of optics, a branch of science that emerged early in the ancient civilizations of Egypt, India,Mesopotamia and Greece is intimately linked to the origins of telescopes.The earliest known use of telescopes dates back to 700 BC, when polished crystal lenses were tested by ancient empires in many parts of the world.

Many mathematicians and physicists from antiquity were instrumental in characterizing the characteristics of light, including reflection and refraction.

Modern scientists were able to create the first telescope in 1608 ,thanks to the efforts of all these discoveries spanning nearly two millennia, when Dutch eyeglass manufacturer Hans Lippershey was able to secure a patent for a refracting telescope.

Though the true inventor is unknown, invention about telescope circulated throughout Europe. After learning of it, Galileo constructed his own version in 1609 and used a telescopic lens to observe celestial objects.

The Greek mathematician Giovanni Demisiani first used the term "telescope" in 1611 to refer to one of Galileo Galilei's instruments that was on display at the Accademia dei Lincei.

Scientists started enhancing telescopes in Europe. After researching optics, Johannes Kepler created a telescope that had two convex lenses, which caused the images to appear upside down. Based on Kepler's works, Isaac Newton constructed a reflecting telescope in 1668 after concluding that mirrors were a preferable material for telescopes than lenses. Astronomy would be dominated by the reflecting telescope centuries later.

The discovery of the first achromatic lens in the middle of the eighteenth century marked a turning point in the history of the modern telescope, allowing for the construction of instruments free from the effects of spherical and chromatic aberration. Following Isaac Newton's initial models, reflecting mirrors also underwent evolution. This was particularly the case with the introduction of silver-coated glass mirrors in the 1850s and aluminized mirrors in the early 1930s.

Scientists were able to investigate space electromagnetic radiation other than light when the radio was developed. The first person to detect radio radiation from space was an American engineer by the name of Karl Jansky in 1931. He discovered a radio interference source emanating from the Milky Way's center. Radio telescopes have since mapped the shape of galaxies and the existence of background microwave radiation.

When telescopes of all sizes and shapes began to be produced in the 20th century, many of them were designed to collect electromagnetic radiation, such as gamma rays, ultraviolet, infrared, and x-rays, rather than visible light.

One of the first telescopes to be launched into space, the Hubble Space Telescope was built and launched in 1990 thanks to a partnership between NASA and the European Space Agency. Hubble is one of the largest and most versatile space telescopes, despite not being the first.

Since being placed into low-Earth orbit, it has participated in numerous important studies. Freed from the distortion caused by Earth's atmosphere and background light, Hubble is able to produce unmatched clear pictures of the stars and planets.

A ground-breaking space telescope was put into service in 1991 to find photons with energies ranging from 20 keV to 30n GeV. Known as the Compton Gamma Ray Observatory (CGRO), it was an X-ray and gamma-ray observatory with four telescopes mounted on a single platform.

The European Space Agency constructed the Herschel Space Observatory, which was operational from 2009 to 2013. It was the biggest infrared telescope ever sent into orbit. The main purpose of the space telescope was to study the coldest and dustiest celestial objects.

Infrared astronomy is the focus of the James Webb Space Telescope (JWST), a space telescope launched in 2021 . Its high-sensitivity and high-resolution instruments enable it to view objects that the Hubble Space Telescope cannot see because they are too faint, old, or far away. This makes it possible to conduct studies in a wide range of astronomical and cosmological domains, including the first star observations, the formation of galaxies, and the in-depth atmospheric characterization of exoplanets that may be habitable.

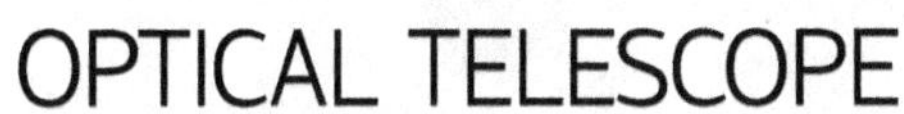

OPTICAL TELESCOPE

OPTICAL TELESCOPE

An optical telescope is one that primarily gathers and concentrates light from the visible portion of the electromagnetic spectrum.The diameter or aperture of an optical telescope's objective, which is its primary lens or mirror that gathers and focuses light, determines how well it can resolve minute details, and the area of the objective determines how well it can gather light. The telescope gathers more light and resolves finer details when the objective is larger.

Three main categories of optical telescopes exist:

Refracting telescopes- which employ prisms (dioptrics) and lenses.

Reflecting telescopes -mirror-based reflecting telescopes.

Catadioptric Telescopes- that combine lenses and mirrors.

Refracting telescopes

An optical telescope that forms an image by using a lens as its objective is known as a refractor, or refracting telescope also called a dioptric telescope.Refracting telescopes usually consist of a lens up front, followed by a long tube and an eyepiece or instrumentation at the back where the view through the telescope is focused.The first kind of optical telescope was a refractor.The same principles apply to all refracting telescopes. In order to focus light , collect more light than the human eye can focus on its own, and provide the viewer with a brighter, clearer, and magnified virtual image , an objective lens and eyepiece are used in tandem.

A refracting telescope's objective bends or refracts light. Parallel light rays converge at a focal point as a result of this refraction, whereas non-parallel light rays converge on a focal plane. The telescope creates a second parallel bundle with angle β by converting a bundle of parallel rays with angle α with the optical axis. The angular magnification is defined as the ratio β/α. It is the same as the ratio of retinal image sizes acquired using and not using a telescope. Refracting telescopes can be configured in a variety of ways to account for aberration and image orientation. These telescopes are known as refracting telescopes or refractors because the image was created by the bending, or refraction, of light.

Evolution of Refracting telescopes

A Galilean telescope is the name given to the design that Galileo Galilei used in 1609.A divergent (plano-concave) eyepiece lens and a convergent (plano-convex) objective lens were employed.A Galilean telescope produces an image that is not inverted and can be made upright with the aid of certain devices because it lacks an intermediary focus in its design.With a total length of 980 millimeters -3 feet 3 inches, Galileo's most potent telescope magnified objects by a factor of 30.A better design than Galileo's was Johannes Kepler's Keplerian telescope, which he created in 1611. Rather than using Galileo's concave eyepiece, it makes use of a convex lens. The converging light rays coming from the eyepiece are an advantage of this arrangement. This gives the viewer an inverted image but permits a much wider field of view and greater eye relief.

The development of the achromatic lens, a multi-element lens that helped reduce chromatic aberration and enabled shorter focal lengths, was the next significant advancement in the evolution of refracting telescopes. Chester Moore Hall, an English barrister, is credited with creating it in 1733. However, John Dollond independently created and patented it sometime in 1758. By using an objective composed of two pieces of glass with different dispersions, "crown" and "flint glass," to reduce chromatic and spherical aberration, the design avoided the need for very long focal lengths in refracting telescopes.

After polishing and grinding each side of the two pieces, they are put together. Achromatic lenses are adjusted to focus two wavelengths in the same plane, usually red and blue.

The Swiss optician Pierre-Louis Guinand created a method in the late 1800s for producing superior quality glass blanks that were larger than four inches.Joseph von Fraunhofer, his apprentice, continued to develop this technology and also created the Fraunhofer doublet lens design . The great refractors of the 19th century were the result of technological advances in glassmaking. These machines grew larger and larger over the course of the decade, reaching a height of over one meter by the century's end. However, silvered-glass reflecting telescopes in astronomy eventually surpassed them in terms of size.

The heliometer, a related device, was first used to determine the distance to another star in the 19th century, when refracting telescopes were employed for groundbreaking work in spectroscopy and astrophotography.

Refracting telescope designs

Most refracting telescopes use two main lenses. The largest lens is called the objective lens, and the smaller lens used for viewing is called the eyepiece lens.

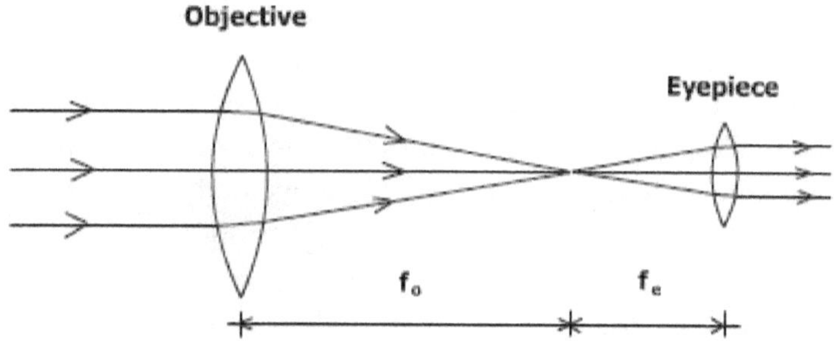

Light in a refracting telescope.

The focal length of a lens determines the size of the image it produces. The image gets larger with a longer focal length. The amount of light that a telescope collects affects how bright an image it produces. The area of the objective lens of a telescope directly relates to its light-gathering power. The telescope can collect more light the larger the lens. The light gathering power increases by a factor of four when the lens's diameter doubles. The extent to which the image light is dispersed determines an image's brightness as well. The image gets brighter the smaller the area.

Chromatic aberration is a kind of image distortion caused by lenses. This happens because different colors are bent at different angles (like in a prism) and focused at different points when light travels through a lens. As a result, stars appear to have rainbow-colored halos around them when viewed through an ordinary lens. A thin lens made of a different type of glass can be placed behind the objective lens to compensate for this.

An apochromat, or apochromatic lens (apo), is a lens that has better correction of chromatic and spherical aberration than the much more common achromat lenses.

The objectives of apochromatic refractors are constructed from unique, extra-low dispersion materials. The three wavelengths that they are intended to focus on in the same plane are usually red, green, and blue. An order of magnitude less can be seen in the residual color error (tertiary spectrum) compared to an achromatic lens.These telescopes produce an extremely sharp image with almost no chromatic aberration because the objective contains fluorite or special extra-low dispersion (ED) glass elements.

When long-exposure photography became available, many astronomical objects were no longer visible due to the modest apertures of refractive telescopes, which did not yield as many discoveries. By then, reflecting telescopes had become more well-known and had surpassed the refractors in terms of peculiarities. In spite of this, a number of discoveries have been made, such as the Moons of Mars, a fifth Moon of Jupiter, and numerous double stars, such as Sirius (the Dog star). Refactors had many applications in terrestrial viewing and photography in addition to positional astronomy.

Using aerial telescopes and single-element objectives, the solar system's moons, including the Galilean moons, were found.

Using a refracting telescope, Galileo Galilei discovered the Galilean satellites of Jupiter in 1610.

Discovered on March 25, 1655, by Dutch astronomer Christiaan Huygens, Titan is the moon of the planet Saturn. Pairs of The 18 and a half-inch Dearborn refracting telescope was used in 1861 to discover a smaller stellar companion for Sirius, the brightest star in the night sky.

By the eighteenth century, reflectors—which could be made quite large and typically did not have the same innate chromatic aberration problem—began to pose a serious threat to refractors. However, doublet refractors with modest apertures were still used by the astronomical community despite the availability of modern instruments. Notable findings include the moons of Mars and Amalthea, Jupiter's fifth moon.

The interstellar medium was one of the discoveries made in 1904 with the aid of the Great Refractor of Potsdam.Calcium was found in the intervening space, according to observations made by astronomer Professor Hartmann of the binary star Mintaka in Orion.

Planet Pluto was discovered by looking at photographs in a blink comparator taken with a refracting telescope, an astrograph.

Yerkes Observatory ,Wisconsin ,USA

The 40-inch (102-cm) Yerkes Observatory refractor is the largest refracting telescope in the world and has been used for scientific and astronomical observation for more than a century.

Though technically larger, the Swedish 1-m Solar Telescope only has 39 inches of clear aperture due to its 43-inch lens diameter. The Meudon Great Refractor and the James Lick Telescope are the next largest refractor telescopes.

Refracting telescopes, which use lenses to gather and focus light, have played a significant role in the history of astronomy and space exploration.

While reflecting telescopes (which use mirrors) are more commonly used in space missions due to their advantages, there have been a few notable missions that employed refracting telescopes.

Here are some space missions that utilized refracting telescopes:

Hubble Space Telescope (HST):

While the Hubble Space Telescope (HST) is primarily known for its reflecting telescope design, it also includes two refracting telescopes as part of its Fine Guidance Sensors (FGS). These FGS instruments are used for precise pointing and stabilization of the telescope and also provide astrometric measurements of celestial objects.

Galileo spacecraft:

The Galileo spacecraft, launched by NASA in 1989, included a refracting telescope as part of its imaging system. The telescope was used to observe Jupiter and its moons during the spacecraft's mission to study the Jovian system. The Galileo spacecraft provided valuable data and images of Jupiter, its moons, and its surrounding environment.

Pioneer Venus Orbiter (PVO):

The Pioneer Venus Orbiter, launched by NASA in 1978, included a refracting telescope as part of its ultraviolet photometer instrument. This telescope was used to study the composition and dynamics of the Venusian atmosphere by measuring UV radiation emitted by the planet. The PVO mission provided important insights into the atmosphere and climate of Venus.

Pioneer 10 and 11:

The Pioneer 10 and 11 spacecraft, launched by NASA in the early 1970s, carried a variety of scientific instruments, including a photopolarimeter that included a refracting telescope. This telescope was used to study the composition and properties of interplanetary dust and to measure the brightness and polarization of stars.

While reflecting telescopes are more commonly used in space missions due to their larger aperture and other advantages, refracting telescopes have been employed in certain spacecraft for specific scientific purposes. These missions have contributed valuable data and observations to our understanding of the solar system and the universe.

Reflecting telescope

Reflectors make up nearly all of the large telescopes used in astronomy research.Reflecting telescopes are capable of producing very large diameter objectives despite producing other kinds of optical aberrations.

A reflecting telescope, also known as a reflector, is a type of telescope that creates images by reflecting light using one or more curved mirrors. Isaac Newton created the reflecting telescope in the 17th century as a replacement for the refracting telescope, which at the time had a serious chromatic aberration problem.

By the turn of the century, a novel technique from the 19th century that involved coating a block of glass with an extremely thin layer of silver had gained popularity. A better reputation for reflecting telescopes was established by the Crossley and Harvard reflecting telescopes, which were the result of common telescopes that had metal mirror designs that were known to have flaws.

Mainly, the metal mirrors tended to tarnish and only reflected roughly 2/3 of the light. Several polishes and tarnishings may cause the mirror to lose its necessary precise figuring.Many reflecting telescope designs have been proposed as a result of the potential benefits of using parabolic mirrors, particularly the reduction of spherical aberration with no chromatic aberration.

Evolution of Reflecting telescopes

The most renowned was James Gregory, who in 1663 published a novel plan for a "reflecting" telescope. The experimental scientist Robert Hooke would have to wait ten years (1673) to construct the kind of telescope that would come to be known as the Gregorian telescope.

Isaac Newton constructed his own reflecting telescope in 1668, which is regarded as the first reflecting telescope.It employed an optical configuration that became known as the Newtonian telescope, consisting of a small diagonal mirror and a metal primary mirror that was spherically ground.

The development of parabolic mirrors in the 18th century, silver coatings for glass mirrors in the 19th century, durable aluminum coatings in the 20th century, segmented mirrors to accommodate larger diameters, and active optics to counteract gravitational deformation were among the many advancements in reflecting telescopes.

Catadioptric telescopes, like the Schmidt camera, are a mid-20th century innovation. They use a spherical mirror and a lens known as a corrector plate as their primary optical elements, and are primarily used for spherically aberration-free wide-field imaging.

Adaptive optics and lucky imaging have been developed in the late 20th century to address vision issues, and reflecting telescopes are a common feature on space telescopes and many other spacecraft imaging devices.

Reflecting telescope designs

Completed by Isaac Newton in 1668, the Newtonian telescope was the first reflecting telescope to be successful. Its primary mirror is typically paraboloid, but at focal ratios of approximately f/10 or longer, a spherical primary mirror may be adequate to provide excellent visual resolution. The light is reflected to a focal plane at the side of the telescope tube's top by a flat secondary mirror. For a given primary size, it is one of the most straightforward and affordable designs, and amateur telescope builders often use it as a home-build project.

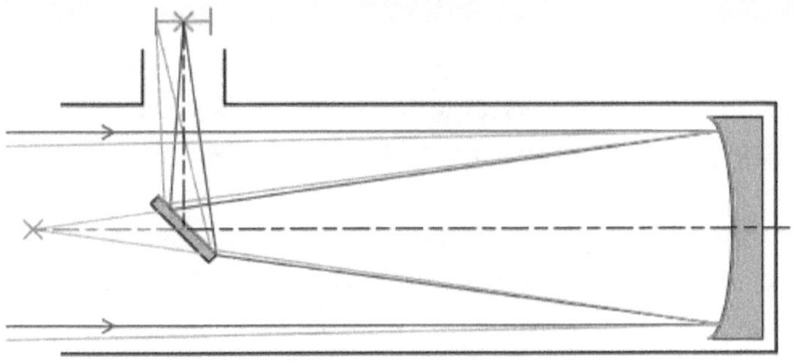

Light path in a Newtonian telescope.

Reflecting telescopes gained immense popularity in astronomy, and this design is used by many well-known telescopes, including the Hubble Space Telescope, as well as numerous popular amateur models. The reflection telescope principle has also been applied to other electromagnetic wavelengths; image-forming optics, for instance, is made possible by the reflection principle in X-ray telescopes.

The Gran Telescopio at Roque de los Muchachos
Observatory, La Palma, Canary Islands

The Gran Telescopio Canarias in the Canary Islands is the largest optical reflector in the world. Its individual mirror segments combine to produce a light-collecting surface equal to 10.4 meters (34 feet) in diameter. Exoplanets, asteroids, comets, and even supernovas have all been studied with it.

The Keck observatory domes , Mauna Kea,Hawaii

The twin Keck telescopes, each measuring 10 meters (33 feet) in diameter, are located not far behind on Hawaii's Mount Kea. They have refined the size of the Andromeda galaxy and obtained the first image of an exoplanet system.

Like any other optical system, reflecting telescopes cannot produce "perfect" images. A reflecting telescope's optical design must always make some compromises in order to image objects at distances up to infinity, view them at different wavelengths of light, and have a means of viewing the image produced by the primary mirror.

Reflecting telescopes, which use mirrors to gather and focus light, are commonly employed in space missions due to their advantages over refracting telescopes.

Reflecting telescopes can be made with larger apertures and are less susceptible to chromatic aberration.

Here are some notable space missions that have utilized reflecting telescopes:

Hubble Space Telescope (HST):

Launched in 1990, the Hubble Space Telescope is one of the most famous and successful space missions in history. It features a 2.4-meter (7.9-foot) diameter reflecting telescope and is equipped with a suite of instruments that observe in various wavelengths, from ultraviolet to near-infrared. Hubble has made numerous groundbreaking discoveries across many fields of astronomy, including cosmology, galactic dynamics, and exoplanet studies.

James Webb Space Telescope (JWST):

Scheduled for launch in late 2021, the James Webb Space Telescope is NASA's next-generation space observatory. It features a large, segmented primary mirror with a diameter of 6.5 meters (21.3 feet), making it the largest space telescope ever built. JWST will observe primarily in the infrared range, enabling it to study the early universe, the formation of galaxies, and the atmospheres of exoplanets.

Spitzer Space Telescope:

Launched in 2003, the Spitzer Space Telescope was designed to observe the universe in the infrared portion of the spectrum. It featured a 0.85-meter (33-inch) diameter reflecting telescope and provided valuable data on a wide range of astrophysical phenomena, including star formation, planetary systems, and the structure of the Milky Way galaxy. Spitzer was retired in 2020 after more than 16 years of operation.

Chandra X-ray Observatory:

Launched in 1999, the Chandra X-ray Observatory is a space telescope designed to observe X-ray emissions from celestial objects such as black holes, neutron stars, and galaxy clusters. It features a high-resolution X-ray mirror assembly with four nested pairs of mirrors. Chandra has revolutionized our understanding of the X-ray universe, revealing dynamic processes and extreme environments.

Fermi Gamma-ray Space Telescope:

Launched in 2008, the Fermi Gamma-ray Space Telescope studies the universe in gamma-ray wavelengths. It features two main instruments, the Large Area Telescope (LAT) and the Gamma-ray Burst Monitor (GBM). The LAT employs a reflecting telescope to detect gamma rays, enabling Fermi to study sources such as pulsars, gamma-ray bursts, and active galactic nuclei.

These space missions demonstrate the versatility and importance of reflecting telescopes in exploring the universe across different wavelengths and phenomena. They have provided invaluable data and insights into the nature of the cosmos, advancing our understanding of fundamental astrophysical processes.

Catadioptric Telescopes

When refraction and reflection are combined in an optical system, typically through the use of curved mirrors (catoptrics) and lenses (dioptrics), the result is a catadioptric optical system.

Catadioptric telescopes are optical instruments that create images by combining mirrors and lenses with precise shapes. This is typically done to allow the telescope to have an aberration-free field of view that is wider and an overall greater degree of error correction than their all-lens or all-mirror counterparts.

Their designs can benefit from a folded optical path, which lowers the mass of the telescope and allows for simple all-spherical surfaces, which will facilitate manufacturing. In a combined image-forming optical system, many types use "correctors," which are lenses or curved mirrors that allow the reflective or refractive element to correct aberrations caused by its counterpart.

Evolution of Catadioptric telescope

The catadioptric telescope, which combines reflecting (mirrors) and refracting (lenses) optics, was created as a result of advances in lens technology outside the field of telescopy, even though both reflecting and refracting models kept getting better over time.

For instance, the renowned catadioptric lighthouse reflector was created in 1820 by physicist Augustin-Jean Fresnel; a microscope was constructed in 1859 by scientist Leon Foucault using catadioptric optics; and the so-called Mangin mirror, which is incorporated into modern catadioptric units, was created in 1876 by officer Alphonse Mangin. Furthermore, the design of modern catadioptric telescopes has been improved by two primary telescope models: the Schupmann medial telescope and the catadioptric dialytes ,the Hamiltonian telescope being the first dialyte unit patented in 1814.

An optician at the Hamburg Observatory in Bergedorf, Germany named Bernhard Schmidt created a catadioptric telescope in 1930 to meet the need for taking pictures of larger celestial regions. With both reflective and refractive optics, a catadioptric telescope combines the best qualities of a reflector and a refractor in one design.

Catadioptric telescope design

The primary mirror of the Schmidt telescope is spherically shaped. Schmidt added a thin lens, known as the correcting plate, at the primary mirror's radius of curvature because parallel light rays reflected by a spherical mirror's center focus light farther away than those reflected from its outer regions. This correcting plate adds very little chromatic aberration because it is so thin.

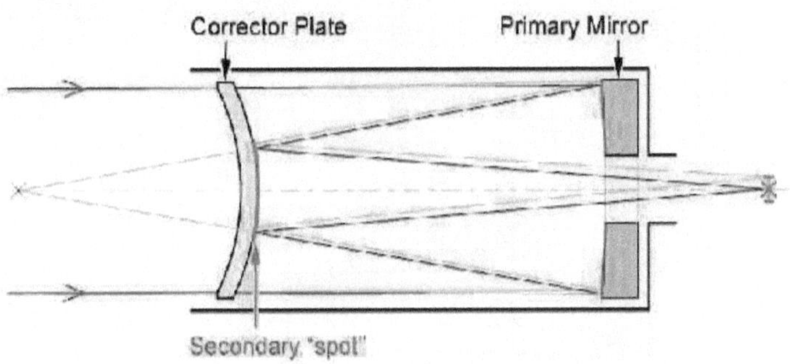

Schmidt camera

Its optical components consist of a simple spherical primary mirror and an aspherical correcting lens, called a Schmidt corrector plate, which is positioned at the primary mirror's center of curvature. The film or other detector is positioned at the prime focus inside the camera. The design is renowned for its ability to control astigmatism and coma while permitting extremely quick focal ratios.

The Schmidt camera is commonly employed as a survey tool for research projects that require extensive coverage of the sky due to its broad field of view. These consist of nova patrols, comet and asteroid searches, and astronomical surveys.

The first relatively large Schmidt telescopes were built at Hamburg Observatory and Palomar Observatory.The telescope used in the Lowell Observatory Near-Earth-Object Search (LONEOS) is also a Schmidt camera. The Schmidt telescope of the Karl Schwarzschild Observatory is the largest Schmidt camera of the world.

Karl Schwarzschild Observatory in Tautenburg, Thuringia, Germany

Catadioptric telescopes, which combine both lenses and mirrors to gather and focus light, have been used in various space missions for their compact design and versatility. Here are some notable space missions that have utilized catadioptric telescopes:

Kepler Space Telescope:

Launched in 2009, the Kepler Space Telescope was designed to search for exoplanets by detecting the tiny dips in brightness as planets pass in front of their host stars. It utilized a catadioptric optical system consisting of a primary mirror and a corrector lens to provide a wide field of view and high photometric precision. Kepler's observations led to the discovery of thousands of exoplanets and revolutionized our understanding of planetary systems.

Coronagraphic missions (e.g., Hubble, JWST):

Various space missions, including the Hubble Space Telescope (HST) and the upcoming James Webb Space Telescope (JWST), have employed coronagraphic instruments for studying faint objects near bright sources. Coronagraphs use a combination of lenses and mirrors to block out the light from a star, revealing nearby objects such as exoplanets or protoplanetary disks. While not strictly catadioptric telescopes themselves, these instruments incorporate catadioptric elements within their optical systems.

Gaia Space Telescope:

Launched in 2013 by the European Space Agency (ESA), the Gaia mission is mapping the positions, distances, and motions of stars in the Milky Way galaxy with unprecedented precision. Gaia's optical system includes mirrors and lenses to focus light onto its large focal plane array of detectors. While not a strictly catadioptric design, Gaia's optical system incorporates both reflective and refractive elements.

ASTERIA (Arcsecond Space Telescope Enabling Research in Astrophysics):

ASTERIA is a NASA CubeSat mission launched in 2017 to demonstrate precision pointing and thermal stability for future space telescopes. It used a catadioptric telescope with a 6.4-centimeter (2.5-inch) aperture and a wide-field camera to observe bright stars and demonstrate high-precision photometry in a small satellite platform.

These examples illustrate the versatility and utility of catadioptric telescopes in various space missions, from exoplanet searches to astrometry and precision pointing demonstrations. Catadioptric designs offer advantages such as compactness, wide fields of view, and aberration correction, making them well-suited for a range of scientific objectives in space exploration.

Telescope Types Working outside the Optical Spectrum

Every celestial object that is warmer than absolute zero releases electromagnetic radiation in some capacity. Scientists use a variety of telescopes to identify the various forms of radiation that are released into the electromagnetic spectrum in order to study the universe. Among them are telescopes for Infrared,Radio, Gamma, X-ray, and Ultraviolet light.

RADIO TELESCOPE

CHAPTER THREE

RADIO TELESCOPE

The primary observational tool in radio astronomy, which examines the radio frequency region of the electromagnetic spectrum emitted by celestial objects, is the radio telescope.

Radio telescopes need very large antennas to gather enough radio energy to study astronomical radio sources, such as planets, stars, nebulas, and galaxies, because their radio waves are very weak due to their great distance from us. They also need very sensitive receiving equipment. The main antennas used in radio telescopes are large parabolic ("dish") antennas.

They can be utilized separately or in an array when electronically connected. In order to prevent electromagnetic interference, radio observatories are ideally situated far from densely populated areas (EMI).

Evolution of Radio telescopes

The evolution of radio telescopes spans over a century and has been marked by significant advancements in technology, observational techniques, and scientific discoveries.

Here's an overview of the key stages in the evolution of radio telescopes:

Early Developments:

Discovery of Cosmic Radio Waves: The development of radio astronomy began in the 1930s when Karl Jansky, an engineer at Bell Telephone Laboratories, detected radio waves coming from the Milky Way. His discovery marked the birth of radio astronomy and paved the way for the construction of specialized telescopes to study cosmic radio emissions.

First Radio Telescope: In 1937, Grote Reber, an amateur radio engineer, built the world's first parabolic radio telescope in his backyard in Wheaton, Illinois. Reber's telescope consisted of a wire mesh dish that focused radio waves onto a receiver, enabling him to create the first radio maps of the sky.

Development of Large Radio Telescopes: In the years following World War II, advances in radar technology and electronics spurred the construction of larger and more sensitive radio telescopes. Organizations such as the US National Radio Astronomy Observatory (NRAO) and the UK's Jodrell Bank Observatory began building large dish antennas for radio astronomy research.

Large radio telescopes were built by universities and research institutions as radio astronomy emerged as a subfield of astronomy as a result of the quick development of radar during World War II. This technology was then applied to radio astronomy.

Interferometry Techniques: In the 1950s, astronomers developed interferometry techniques to combine signals from multiple smaller telescopes, effectively creating a virtual telescope with the resolution of a much larger instrument. Interferometric arrays such as the Cambridge

Interferometer and the Westerbork Synthesis Radio Telescope (WSRT) allowed astronomers to achieve high-resolution radio imaging.

Radio Telescope Designs:

Radio telescopes come in various designs depending on their intended purpose, observing frequencies, and location. Here are some common designs:

Parabolic Dish Antennas:

These are the most common type of radio telescopes. They consist of a large dish-shaped reflecting surface (often made of metal) that focuses incoming radio waves onto a receiver placed above the dish's focal point. The size of the dish determines the telescope's sensitivity and resolution.

Examples include the Arecibo Observatory and the Green Bank Telescope.

The Green Bank Telescope,United States

Synthesis Arrays:

The Very Large Array radio telescope located near
Socorro, New Mexico.

These consist of multiple smaller antennas spread out over a large area, working together to simulate a single, larger telescope. By combining signals from all antennas using a technique called interferometry, synthesis arrays can achieve high resolution and sensitivity. Examples include the Very Large Array (VLA) in New Mexico and the Atacama Large Millimeter/submillimeter Array (ALMA) in Chile.

Aperture Arrays:

These telescopes use an array of small, fixed antennas without any moving parts. The signals from these antennas are combined electronically to simulate a single large dish. Aperture arrays are often used in low-frequency radio astronomy due to their cost-effectiveness and ability to cover large areas of the sky. The Low-Frequency Array (LOFAR) in Europe is an example of such a telescope.

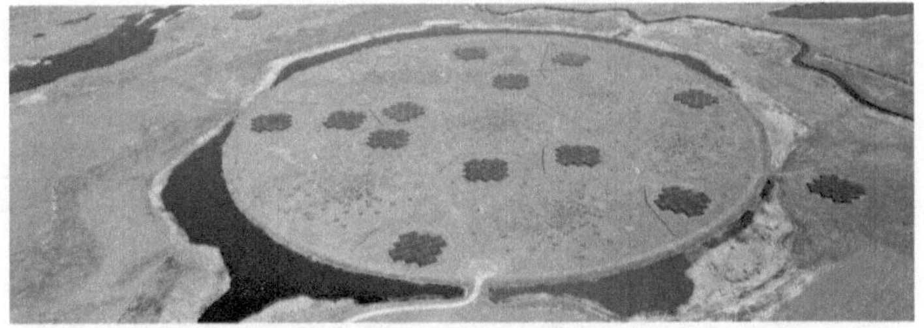

Low-Frequency Array (LOFAR)

Steerable Antennas:

The Karl G. Jansky Very Large Array (VLA)

Some radio telescopes are designed with movable antennas that can be pointed at different parts of the sky. These telescopes often have a parabolic dish or an array of antennas mounted on a rotating platform or on tracks. The ability to steer the antennas allows astronomers to observe different celestial objects throughout the night. The Karl G. Jansky Very Large Array (VLA) and the Australia

Telescope Compact Array (ATCA) are examples of steerable radio telescopes.

Spherical Reflectors:

The 100-m radio telescope Effelsberg near Bad Münstereifel.

These telescopes use a spherical reflecting surface instead of a parabolic one. While less common, they have certain advantages in terms of ease of construction and cost. One example is the Radio Telescope Effelsberg in Germany.

Single-Dish vs. Interferometric Arrays:

Some radio telescopes operate as single dishes, collecting radio waves and focusing them directly onto a receiver. Others operate as interferometric arrays, combining signals from multiple antennas to achieve higher resolution. The choice between these designs depends on the specific goals of the telescope and the scientific questions it aims to address.

Each design has its advantages and limitations, and astronomers select the appropriate type of telescope based on the scientific questions they want to investigate, the desired sensitivity and resolution, and budgetary constraints.

The electromagnetic spectrum, which comprises the radio spectrum, has a very wide range of frequencies. As a result, there is a great deal of variation in the size, shape, and design of the antennas used as radio telescopes. They are typically large stationary reflectors with movable focal points or directional antenna arrays akin to "TV antennas" operating at wavelengths between 30 and 3 meters (10–100 MHz). These kinds of antennas can be used to observe wavelengths that are so long that coarse wire mesh can be used to create the "reflector" surfaces.

Shorter wavelengths are primarily used with parabolic "dish" antennas. The ratio of the dish's diameter to the wavelength of the radio waves being observed determines the angular resolution of a dish antenna. This determines what size radio telescope dish is required for a practical resolution. The typical diameter of radio telescopes operating at wavelengths between 3 meters and 30 cm (100 MHz and 1 GHz) is well over 100 meters. The diameter of telescopes operating at wavelengths shorter than 30 cm (above 1 GHz) varies from 3 to 90 meters.

The invention of astronomical interferometry in 1946—a method of combining signals from several antennas to simulate a larger antenna in order to achieve higher resolution—was one of the most significant advancements. Arrays of parabolic dishes, arrays of one-dimensional antennas or two-dimensional arrays of omnidirectional dipoles, are the typical components of astronomical radio interferometers. The array's telescopes are all widely spaced apart and are typically connected by optical fiber, coaxial cable, waveguide, or other transmission lines.

The stability of electronic oscillators has improved recently, making it possible to perform interferometry by independently recording the signals at each antenna and then correlating the recordings at a central processing facility. VLBI, or Very Long Baseline Interferometry, is the term for this process. Although interferometry collects more signals overall, its main goal is to significantly increase resolution by using an approach known as aperture synthesis. The way this technique operates is by superposing (interfering) the signal waves from the various telescopes according to the idea that two waves with opposite phases will cancel each other out, while waves that coincide with the same phase will add to each other.

This results in a combined telescope with the resolution (but not the sensitivity) of a single antenna whose diameter is equal to the distance between the antennas in the array that are furthest apart.Many distinct separations between telescopes are needed to produce an image of high quality. A baseline is the projected distance, as seen from the radio source, between any two telescopes. Using 27 telescopes and 351 independent baselines simultaneously, the Very Large Array (VLA) near Socorro, New Mexico, for instance, can achieve a resolution of 0.2 arc seconds at 3 cm wavelengths.

The largest array, the Low-Frequency Array (LOFAR), was completed in 2012 and is situated in western Europe. It operates between 1.25 and 30 m wavelengths and is made up of about 81,000 small antennas spread across 48 stations over an area several hundred kilometers in diameter. Postobservation processing VLBI systems have been built with antennas thousands of miles apart. In-depth pictures of the Cosmic Microwave Background's polarization and anisotropies have also been captured using radio interferometers.

The Five-hundred-meter Aperture Spherical Telescope (FAST), completed by China in 2016, is the largest filled-aperture i.e., full dish radio telescope in the world. The 500-meter-diameter (1,600-foot) dish is situated within a naturally occurring karst depression in the landscape, encompassing an area equivalent to thirty football fields.
A computer is used to control 4,450 movable panels that make up the active dish. The telescope can be steered to point at any point up to 40° from the zenith by adjusting the shape of the dish and shifting the feed cabin on its cables.

Five-hundred-meter Aperture Spherical Telescope (FAST)

The RATAN-600, a 576-meter circle of rectangular radio reflectors that can all be aimed toward a central conical receiver, is the largest single radio telescope of any kind. It is situated close to Nizhny Arkhyz, Russia.

The aforementioned stationary dishes are not completely "steerable"; they are limited to aiming at specific locations in the sky close to the zenith and are unable to receive data from sources close to the horizon. The 100-meter Green Bank Telescope in West Virginia, USA, is the largest fully steerable dish radio telescope. The Effelsberg 100-m Radio Telescope, run by the Max Planck Institute for Radio Astronomy near Bonn, Germany, is the largest fully steerable radio telescope in Europe. For thirty years prior to the construction of the Green Bank antenna, it was also the largest fully steerable telescope in the world.The 76-meter Lovell Telescope, completed in 1957 at Jodrell Bank Observatory in Cheshire, England, is the third-largest fully steerable radio telescope.

Six 70-meter dishes—three in the NASA Deep Space Network and three Russian RT-70s—make up the fourth-largest fully steerable radio telescope.

The Ooty Radio Telescope,South India has been designed and fabricated with domestic Indian technological resources. The ORT was completed in 1970 and continues to be one of the most sensitive radio telescopes in the world.

Ooty Radio Telescope,South India

The Ooty Radio Telescope,South India has been designed and fabricated with domestic Indian technological resources. The ORT was completed in 1970 and continues to be one of the most sensitive radio telescopes in the world.

Observations made using this telescope have led to important discoveries and to explain various phenomena occurring in the Solar System and in other celestial bodies.

The reflecting surface of the telescope is made of 1,100 thin stainless-steel wires running parallel to each other for the entire length of the cylinder and supported on 24 steerable parabolic frames.

An array of 1,056 half-wave dipoles in front of a 90-degree corner reflector forms the primary feed of the telescope.

Space missions utilizing radio telescopes have significantly contributed to our understanding of the universe in the radio wavelength range, revealing insights into various astrophysical phenomena. Here are some notable space missions that have employed radio telescopes:

1. RadioAstron:

- Launched in 2011, RadioAstron is a Russian-led space mission that operates in conjunction with ground-based radio telescopes to form a space-based interferometer. It features a 10-meter (33-foot) radio telescope aboard the Spektr-R spacecraft, which is used to observe celestial objects at centimeter and millimeter wavelengths. RadioAstron has achieved the highest angular resolution in radio astronomy to date, allowing it to study phenomena such as active galactic nuclei, pulsars, and star formation with unprecedented detail.

2. HALCA (Highly Advanced Laboratory for Communications and Astronomy):

- HALCA was a Japanese space mission launched in 1997 as part of the VLBI (Very Long Baseline Interferometry) Space Observatory Program. It featured an 8-meter (26-foot) radio telescope and operated in conjunction with ground-based radio telescopes to conduct high-resolution observations at centimeter wavelengths. HALCA contributed to studies of quasars, cosmic jets, and other radio-emitting sources.

3. Radio JOVE:

- Radio JOVE is an educational project that provides students and amateur astronomers with the opportunity to observe and study radio emissions from Jupiter and the Sun. Participants build their own simple radio telescopes based on designs provided by the project and use them to detect and analyze radio signals from celestial objects. While not a dedicated space mission, Radio JOVE engages enthusiasts in radio astronomy and contributes to public outreach and education.

4. Planck Space Observatory:

- Launched in 2009 by the European Space Agency (ESA), the Planck Space Observatory was primarily designed to study the cosmic microwave background (CMB) radiation, the relic radiation from the Big Bang. While not a radio telescope in the traditional sense, Planck's instruments operated at microwave frequencies, overlapping with the lower end of the radio spectrum. Planck provided high-resolution maps of the CMB, yielding valuable insights into the early universe's structure, composition, and evolution.

These space missions demonstrate the importance of radio telescopes in exploring the universe across a wide range of wavelengths and phenomena. They have provided invaluable data and observations that have advanced our understanding of astrophysical processes, cosmology, and the nature of the cosmos.

INFRARED TELESCOPE

CHAPTER FOUR

INFRARED TELESCOPE

A telescope that detects celestial bodies through the use of infrared light is called an infrared telescope. An infrared telescope is a device used to identify and analyze infrared radiation from objects outside of Earth's atmosphere, such as gas and dust in other galaxies, nebulae, and young stars.

Reflecting telescopes intended for visible light observations and infrared telescopes are not very different from one another. Since infrared photons have lower energies than visible light, the primary distinction between the two types is the location of the infrared telescope. The majority of the water vapor in the Earth's atmosphere is found in the lower atmospheric regions, or close to sea level, where it is easily absorbed by infrared radiation. Infrared telescopes that are confined to Earth have been effectively positioned atop tall mountains, such as Mauna Kea in Hawaii.

There are three types of infrared telescopes: Terrestrial, Aerial, and Space-based. They have an infrared camera that needs to be cooled to cryogenic temperatures, along with a unique solid-state infrared detector.

Infrared telescopes are astronomical instruments designed to observe celestial objects in the infrared portion of the electromagnetic spectrum, which lies between visible light and microwave radiation. These telescopes are crucial for studying objects that emit primarily in the infrared, such as cool stars, interstellar dust clouds, protoplanetary disks, and distant galaxies. Here are the key components and characteristics of infrared telescopes:

Optical Design:

Primary Mirror or Lens: Like optical telescopes, infrared telescopes use mirrors or lenses to collect and focus incoming light. The primary mirror or lens gathers infrared radiation from celestial objects and directs it to the telescope's focal plane.

Secondary Mirrors : In some telescopes, secondary mirrors are used to further focus or direct the light onto detectors or instruments.

Instruments and Detectors:

Infrared Sensors and Detectors: Infrared telescopes are equipped with specialized detectors that are sensitive to infrared radiation. These detectors can be made from materials such as indium antimonide (InSb), mercury cadmium telluride (HgCdTe), or other semiconductor compounds. They convert incoming infrared radiation into electrical signals that can be processed and analyzed by computers.

Spectrographs: Many infrared telescopes are equipped with spectrographs, which disperse infrared light into its component wavelengths. Infrared spectroscopy allows astronomers to study the chemical composition, temperature, and physical properties of celestial objects.

Imagers: Infrared imagers capture images of celestial objects in the infrared range. They are used to study the structure, morphology, and distribution of infrared-emitting sources, such as star-forming regions and galaxies.

Cooling Systems:

Cryogenic Cooling: To reduce thermal noise and increase sensitivity, many infrared telescopes and detectors are cooled to cryogenic temperatures using liquid helium or mechanical coolers. Cryogenic cooling minimizes the infrared emission from the telescope itself, allowing for more sensitive observations of faint infrared sources.

Infrared space observations were first made with ground-based telescopes. The mid-1960s saw a rise in their popularity. The majority of infrared light is strongly absorbed by carbon dioxide and water vapor in the Earth's atmosphere, therefore ground-based infrared astronomy is only possible at short wavelengths where atmospheric absorption is less intense.Because infrared radiation is absorbed by water vapor in the Earth's atmosphere, ground-based telescopes are limited in their capabilities. To increase visibility, ground-based infrared telescopes are typically positioned in arid climates and atop tall mountains.

Scientists raised the altitude of infrared telescopes with balloons in the 1960s. They could travel up to a height of roughly 25 miles (40 kilometers) using balloons. Infrared telescopes were mounted atop rockets in 1967. The earliest infrared telescopes were mounted in the air. Since then, infrared telescopes have been carried by aircraft such as the Kuiper Airborne Observatory (KAO).

NASA's Stratospheric Observatory for Infrared Astronomy (SOFIA) was the most recent airborne infrared telescope to reach the stratosphere, having done so in May 2010. Its ability to observe from high altitudes and its mobility make it an invaluable asset for exploring the universe in the infrared.A 17-ton infrared telescope was mounted on a Boeing 747 jet plane by scientists from the German Aerospace Center and the United States.

NASA's Stratospheric Observatory for Infrared Astronomy (SOFIA)

By putting infrared telescopes in orbit, Earth's atmosphere's interference is removed. The first space telescope to survey the whole night sky at infrared wavelengths was the Infrared Astronomical Satellite (IRAS).Its mission, which began on January 25, 1983, lasted for ten months.During its operations, more than a quarter of a million distinct targets were observed, both inside and outside the Solar System.Furthermore, new objects such as comets and asteroids were found.It provided information about other galaxies as well as the Milky Way, our galaxy's central region.

The Wide-field Infrared Survey Explorer (WISE) is an infrared telescope that NASA is currently using on solar-powered spacecraft in orbit.Launched in December 2009, the Wide-field Infrared Survey Explorer (WISE, also known as observatory code C51, Explorer 92, and SMEX-6) is a NASA space telescope dedicated to infrared astronomy as part of the Explorers Program.Numerous star clusters and thousands of minor planets were found by WISE. Additionally, its observations confirmed the detection of the first Earth trojan asteroid and brown dwarf of the Y type.

Wide-field Infrared Survey Explorer -WISE

Infrared astronomy is the focus of the James Webb Space Telescope (JWST), a space telescope.The primary purpose of Webb is near-infrared astronomy. One important method for doing this is to observe in the infrared spectrum, which better penetrates obscuring dust and gas due to cosmological redshift. This makes it possible to observe colder, dimmer objects.

Webb, which in launched in December 2021 on an Ariane 5 rocket from Europe's Spaceport in French Guiana, is intended to provide astronomers with the tools they need to advance their understanding in a variety of astronomical fields. This includes studying our own Solar System, how stars and planets form, including planets outside of it, exoplanets, and how galaxies form and change in ways that have never been possible before.

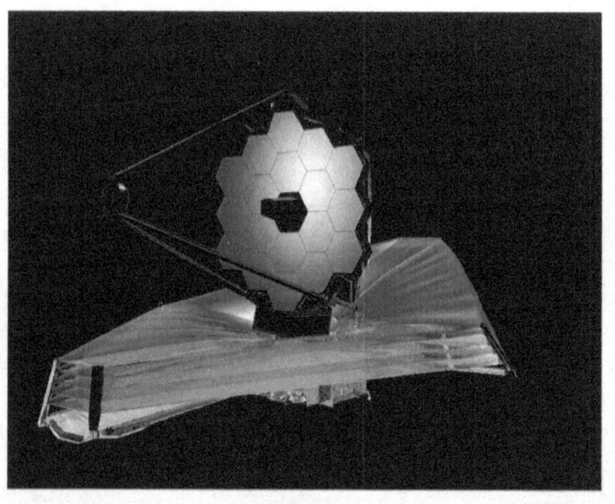

James Webb Space Telescope (JWST)

An international project headed by NASA in collaboration with ESA and the Canadian Space Agency is the James Webb Space Telescope.Webb, an infrared telescope, will investigate scientific issues to learn more about the universe's beginnings and our role in it.Compared to Hubble, JWST can see a far wider range of the infrared spectrum and gathers six times as much light. As the newest premier space observatory in the world, it expands and enhances Hubble's observations.

Several other space missions have employed infrared telescopes to observe the universe in the infrared portion of the electromagnetic spectrum. Infrared observations are crucial for studying cooler objects such as dust clouds, molecular clouds, protoplanetary disks, and distant galaxies. Here are some notable space missions that have utilized infrared telescopes:

1. Spitzer Space Telescope:

- Launched in 2003 by NASA, the Spitzer Space Telescope was specifically designed to observe the universe in the infrared range. It featured a 0.85-meter (33-inch) diameter reflecting telescope and several instruments operating at wavelengths from 3 to 180 micrometers. Spitzer provided valuable data on star formation, exoplanets, the interstellar medium, and distant galaxies before being decommissioned in 2020.

2. Herschel Space Observatory:

- Launched in 2009 by the European Space Agency (ESA), the Herschel Space Observatory was the largest infrared telescope ever launched into space. It featured a 3.5-meter (11.5-foot) diameter reflecting telescope and observed in far-infrared and submillimeter wavelengths. Herschel provided unprecedented insights into star formation, galaxy evolution, and the composition of interstellar dust before concluding its mission in 2013.

3. Akari (ASTRO-F):

- Launched in 2006 by the Japan Aerospace Exploration Agency (JAXA), Akari was an infrared astronomical satellite that conducted an all-sky survey in infrared wavelengths. It featured a 68.5-centimeter (27-inch) diameter reflecting telescope and provided valuable data on the infrared sky, including observations of galaxies, stars, and interstellar dust.

These space missions have significantly advanced our understanding of the universe by providing unique observations in the infrared portion of the spectrum. They have revealed new insights into the formation and evolution of stars, galaxies, and planetary systems, as well as the composition and structure of the interstellar medium.

X RAY TELESCOPE

CHAPTER FIVE

X RAY TELESCOPE

X-ray telescopes are designed to observe X-rays emitted by extremely hot and energetic objects in the universe, such as black holes, neutron stars, and active galactic nuclei. Traditional optical telescopes are not capable of detecting X-rays because X-rays have much higher energy and shorter wavelengths than visible light. Therefore, X-ray telescopes use different techniques to collect and focus X-rays onto detectors.

Mirrors do not reflect visible light the same way that they do for X-rays. X-ray photons are extremely energetic, and as such, they enter the mirror similarly to how bullets enter a wall. X-rays will also bounce off mirrors in the same way that bullets do when they strike a wall at a grazing angle (see diagram below). Because of these characteristics, X-ray telescopes need to differ greatly from optical telescopes.

The mirrors must be positioned exactly parallel to the incoming X-rays and with their shapes exact. As a result, they resemble barrels rather than the recognizable dish shape of optical telescopes.

A group of scientists led by Riccardo Giacconi at American Science and Engineering in Cambridge, Massachusetts created the first imaging X-ray telescope.

In 1963, it was launched on a tiny sounding rocket and produced rudimentary pictures of hot spots in the Sun's upper atmosphere.

X-ray observatories have to be positioned far above the surface of the Earth because X-rays are absorbed by the atmosphere. This means that in order to transmit data back to Earth, the highly developed electronics and mirrors that are incredibly precise must be able to survive the harsh conditions of space and the stresses of a rocket launch.

When radiation detectors on board rockets were momentarily carried above the atmosphere in 1949, they discovered X-rays emanating from the Sun, providing the first indication that cosmic X-rays exist. It was over ten years before X-rays from extrasolar sources were detected by a much better detector.

Components of X-ray Telescopes:

Primary Mirror (or Optics):

Unlike optical telescopes that use lenses or mirrors to focus visible light, X-ray telescopes use mirrors coated with special materials that can reflect X-rays. These mirrors are typically made of materials such as nickel, gold, or iridium.The primary mirror is usually parabolic or hyperbolic in shape to focus incoming X-rays onto a focal point.

Secondary Mirror (or Optics):

In some X-ray telescope designs, a secondary mirror is used to further focus and direct the X-rays onto a detector.The secondary mirror is positioned in the path of the focused X-rays reflected by the primary mirror, redirecting them towards the detector.

Detector:

X-ray detectors are crucial components of X-ray telescopes. They convert incoming X-rays into electronic signals that can be processed and analyzed.Common types of X-ray detectors include charge-coupled devices (CCDs), complementary metal-oxide-semiconductor (CMOS) detectors, and X-ray sensitive films.

The detector records the intensity and spatial distribution of X-rays, allowing astronomers to create images and analyze the properties of celestial objects emitting X-rays.

Functioning of X-ray Telescopes:

Collecting X-rays:

X-ray telescopes are typically placed in space or at high-altitude locations to avoid absorption and scattering of X-rays by Earth's atmosphere.

As X-rays enter the telescope's field of view, they interact with the mirrors' specially coated surfaces, which reflect and focus them towards the focal point.

Focusing X-rays:

The primary mirror's shape is designed to focus X-rays onto a specific focal point. Due to the short wavelengths of X-rays, precise mirror surfaces are necessary to achieve accurate focusing.

Some X-ray telescope designs may incorporate multiple nested mirrors or mirror segments to increase collecting area and improve focusing efficiency.

Detecting X-rays:

The focused X-rays are directed onto the detector, where they interact with the detector material, causing it to produce electrical signals proportional to the X-ray intensity.

These signals are then amplified, digitized, and processed to create images and spectra of the observed X-ray sources.

X-ray telescopes often employ sophisticated data processing techniques to enhance image quality, remove background noise, and extract valuable scientific information from the detected X-ray signals.

Illustrative Diagram of an X-ray Telescope:

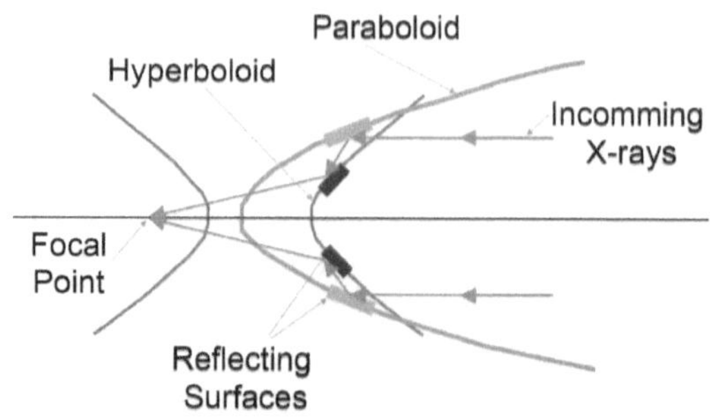

Basic components and functioning of an X-ray telescope

This diagram illustrates the basic components and functioning of an X-ray telescope, including the primary mirror, secondary mirror, and detector assembly.

In summary, X-ray telescopes play a crucial role in studying high-energy phenomena in the universe, providing astronomers with valuable insights into the nature and behavior of celestial objects emitting X-rays.

Several major X-ray astronomy missions have been launched over the years, each contributing significantly to our understanding of the universe's high-energy phenomena. Here are some notable X-ray astronomy missions:

1. Einstein Observatory (HEAO-2):
- Launched in 1978, the Einstein Observatory was the first fully imaging X-ray telescope put into space.

- It provided high-resolution X-ray images of celestial objects and conducted surveys across the entire sky, greatly advancing X-ray astronomy.

2. ROSAT (Röntgensatellit):

- Launched in 1990 by NASA and the German Aerospace Center (DLR), ROSAT was a German-led X-ray observatory.

- ROSAT performed the first deep all-sky survey in the X-ray band, discovering thousands of X-ray sources.

- It also conducted targeted observations of specific objects, including stars, galaxies, and clusters of galaxies.

3. Chandra X-ray Observatory:

- Launched by NASA in 1999, the Chandra X-ray Observatory is one of the most powerful X-ray telescopes ever built.

- Chandra has provided unprecedented high-resolution images of X-ray sources, including black holes, neutron stars, supernova remnants, and galaxy clusters.

- It has made significant contributions to various fields of astrophysics, including black hole physics, galaxy evolution, and the study of dark matter.

4. XMM-Newton (X-ray Multi-Mirror Mission):

- Launched by the European Space Agency (ESA) in 1999, XMM-Newton is a space observatory designed for X-ray astronomy.

- XMM-Newton has a large collecting area and is equipped with three X-ray telescopes and a suite of scientific instruments.

- It has conducted deep surveys of the X-ray universe, studied X-ray binaries, active galactic nuclei, and clusters of galaxies, among other targets.

5. Swift Gamma-Ray Burst Mission:

- Launched in 2004 by NASA in collaboration with

international partners, Swift is primarily designed to study gamma-ray bursts (GRBs).

- Swift's X-ray Telescope (XRT) observes the afterglows of GRBs and other transient events in the X-ray band, providing crucial insights into the physics of these energetic phenomena.

6. NuSTAR (Nuclear Spectroscopic Telescope Array):
- Launched by NASA in 2012, NuSTAR is the first focusing X-ray telescope to operate in the high-energy X-ray band (up to 79 keV).
- NuSTAR has exceptional sensitivity to hard X-rays, allowing it to study black holes, neutron stars, supernova remnants, and other high-energy sources with unprecedented detail.

7. Astro-H / Hitomi:
- Launched by JAXA (Japan Aerospace Exploration Agency) in 2016, Astro-H, renamed Hitomi, was an X-ray observatory designed to study the high-energy universe.
- Despite a premature end to its mission due to a malfunction, Hitomi provided valuable data on galaxy clusters, supernova remnants, and other astrophysical phenomena during its brief operational period.

These missions, along with others, have significantly advanced our understanding of the universe's X-ray emission, shedding light on some of the most energetic processes and objects in the cosmos.

GAMMA-RAY TELESCOPE

GAMMA-RAY TELESCOPE

Scientists knew that the universe should be producing gamma rays long before experiments could detect them emitted by cosmic sources. Researchers Eugene Feenberg and Henry Primakoff (1948), Sachio Hayakawa and I.B. Hutchinson (1952), and Philip Morrison (1958) in particular had led scientists to believe that gamma-ray emission would be the product of several processes occurring in the universe.

These processes included interactions of energetic electrons with magnetic fields, supernova explosions, and cosmic rays with interstellar gas. But ability to actually detect these emissions did not develop until the 1960s.Since Earth's atmosphere absorbs the majority of gamma rays from space, gamma-ray astronomy could not advance until balloons and spacecraft could raise detectors above all or most of the atmosphere.

They suggested a uniform "gamma-ray background" because they seemed to originate from every direction in the universe. The interaction of interstellar gas with cosmic rays, which are extremely energetic charged particles in space, would be expected to produce such a background.

It was not possible to observe gamma rays until the 1960s. Compared to X-rays or visible light, gamma rays are much harder to observe because they are much rarer—even a "bright" source requires several minutes of observation before it is detected—and they are also more difficult to focus, which leads to very low resolution.

Gamma-ray telescopes are specialized instruments designed to observe gamma rays, the highest-energy form of electromagnetic radiation. Gamma rays originate from some of the most energetic phenomena in the universe, such as supernova explosions, black holes, and gamma-ray bursts. Traditional telescopes cannot detect gamma rays due to their high energy and penetrating nature, so gamma-ray telescopes employ different techniques to observe them.

Components of Gamma-ray Telescopes:
Detector System:
Gamma-ray detectors are the primary components of gamma-ray telescopes. They are designed to detect individual gamma-ray photons and measure their energies.Common types of gamma-ray detectors include scintillation detectors, solid-state detectors, and gas-filled detectors.These detectors convert incoming gamma-ray photons into detectable signals, typically through interactions that produce light pulses or electrical signals proportional to the gamma-ray energy.

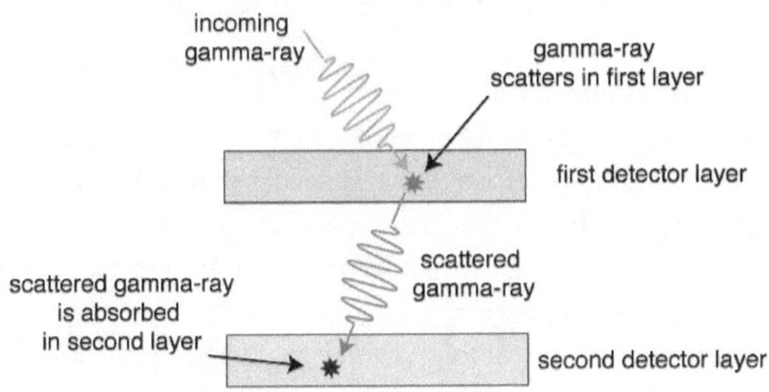

Gamma Ray detector

Collimation System:

Gamma-ray telescopes often incorporate collimation systems to help determine the direction of incoming gamma rays.Collimators are devices that restrict the field of view of the telescope, allowing it to focus on specific regions of the sky.

By measuring the arrival direction of gamma rays, astronomers can pinpoint the locations of gamma-ray sources with high precision.

Data Processing and Analysis:

Gamma-ray telescopes generate vast amounts of data that require sophisticated processing and analysis techniques.

Data from gamma-ray detectors are processed to reconstruct the energy, arrival direction, and arrival time of detected gamma rays.Analysis methods include image reconstruction, spectral analysis, and correlation with observations in other wavelengths to identify gamma-ray sources and study their properties.

Functioning of Gamma-ray Telescopes:

Detecting Gamma Rays:
Gamma-ray telescopes are typically placed in space or at high-altitude locations to avoid absorption and scattering of gamma rays by Earth's atmosphere.As gamma rays enter the telescope's field of view, they interact with the detector system, producing detectable signals.

Each gamma-ray photon's energy is measured by the detector, providing information about the gamma-ray source's characteristics.

Determining Source Positions:
The collimation system helps determine the directions from which gamma rays arrive.By analyzing the arrival directions of gamma rays detected by the telescope, astronomers can map the positions of gamma-ray sources in the sky.

Gamma-ray Sources:
Gamma-ray telescopes observe a wide range of celestial objects and phenomena, including active galactic nuclei, pulsars, gamma-ray bursts, and supernova remnants.By studying the gamma-ray emission from these sources, astronomers can investigate the underlying physical processes, such as particle acceleration, nuclear reactions, and extreme environments associated with these objects.

Fermi Gamma-ray Space Telescope

The Fermi Gamma-ray Space Telescope, launched by NASA in 2008, is an example of a gamma-ray telescope that has made significant contributions to gamma-ray astronomy.

Several missions have been dedicated to gamma-ray astronomy, aiming to observe and study high-energy phenomena in the universe. Here are some notable gamma-ray telescopes and missions:

Fermi Gamma-ray Space Telescope (formerly GLAST):

Launched by NASA in 2008, the Fermi Gamma-ray Space Telescope is a space observatory designed to study gamma rays in the energy range from 8 keV to more than 300 GeV.

Fermi carries two main instruments: the Large Area Telescope (LAT) for detecting gamma rays over a wide energy range and the Gamma-ray Burst Monitor (GBM) for detecting gamma-ray bursts (GRBs).Fermi has made significant contributions to various fields of gamma-ray astronomy, including the study of active galactic nuclei, pulsars, gamma-ray bursts, and dark matter.

Compton Gamma Ray Observatory (CGRO):

Launched by NASA in 1991, CGRO was the second of NASA's Great Observatories. It operated until 2000.

CGRO carried four main instruments: the Burst and Transient Source Experiment (BATSE), the Oriented Scintillation Spectrometer Experiment (OSSE), the Imaging Compton Telescope (COMPTEL), and the Energetic Gamma Ray Experiment Telescope (EGRET).

CGRO made groundbreaking discoveries in gamma-ray astronomy, including the identification of gamma-ray bursts as coming from distant galaxies, the detection of gamma-ray emission from pulsars, and the study of gamma-ray sources across the sky.

INTEGRAL (INTErnational Gamma-Ray Astrophysics Laboratory):

Launched by the European Space Agency (ESA) in 2002, INTEGRAL is a space observatory designed to observe gamma rays with energies from 15 keV to 10 MeV.INTEGRAL carries four main instruments: the Spectrometer on INTEGRAL (SPI), the Imager on Board the INTEGRAL Satellite (IBIS), the Joint European X-ray Monitor (JEM-X), and the Optical Monitoring Camera (OMC).INTEGRAL has contributed to the study of gamma-ray bursts, black hole binaries, galactic nuclei, and other high-energy phenomena.INTEGRAL continues to operate and provide valuable insights into the gamma-ray universe, expanding our understanding of the most extreme and energetic phenomena in the cosmos

AGILE (Astro-rivelatore Gamma a Immagini Leggero):

Launched by the Italian Space Agency (ASI) in 2007, AGILE is a small space mission dedicated to gamma-ray astrophysics.AGILE carries two main instruments: the Gamma-ray Imaging Detector (GRID) and the Mini-Calorimeter (MCAL).

AGILE has focused on the study of gamma-ray bursts, blazars, pulsars, and other sources of high-energy gamma rays.

VERITAS (Very Energetic Radiation Imaging Telescope Array System):

VERITAS is a ground-based gamma-ray observatory located at the Fred Lawrence Whipple Observatory in Arizona, USA.VERITAS consists of an array of four imaging atmospheric Cherenkov telescopes (IACTs) designed to detect gamma rays with energies above about 100 GeV.VERITAS contributes to the study of gamma-ray sources, including active galactic nuclei, supernova remnants, and gamma-ray bursts.

These missions, both space-based and ground-based, have significantly advanced our understanding of the universe's high-energy phenomena through gamma-ray observations. They have provided crucial insights into the nature of gamma-ray sources and the physical processes driving their emission.

In conclusion, gamma-ray telescopes are essential for understanding the universe's most energetic phenomena. By identifying and examining gamma-ray emission from celestial objects, astronomers can learn more about the harsh conditions and mechanisms that power the most potent energy sources in the universe.

ULTRA VIOLET TELESCOPE

CHAPTER SEVEN

ULTRA VIOLET TELESCOPE

The signature of hotter objects, usually in the early and late phases of their evolution, is ultraviolet radiation. When viewed in ultraviolet light, the majority of stars in the Earth's sky would lose prominence. It would be possible to see some extremely young massive stars as well as some extremely old stars and galaxies that are becoming hotter and releasing higher-energy radiation as they approach or pass away. Along the Milky Way, gas and dust clouds would obstruct vision in numerous directions.

An ultraviolet telescope is a specialized astronomical instrument designed to observe celestial objects in the ultraviolet (UV) portion of the electromagnetic spectrum. These telescopes are crucial tools for studying phenomena that emit UV radiation, such as hot stars, active galaxies, and certain types of nebulae.

How Ultraviolet Telescopes Work:

UV Sensitivity: Ultraviolet telescopes are equipped with detectors that are sensitive to UV radiation. Unlike our eyes, which cannot detect UV light, these detectors can capture and record the faint UV signals emitted by celestial objects.

Filters and Optics: Ultraviolet telescopes often use specialized filters and optics to focus and isolate UV light. UV-transparent materials such as magnesium fluoride or lithium fluoride are used in the telescope's optics to allow UV light to pass through while filtering out other wavelengths.

Observing Techniques: Observing in the ultraviolet range presents unique challenges due to the absorption of UV light by Earth's atmosphere. To overcome this limitation, many UV telescopes are placed in space, above Earth's atmosphere, where they can observe celestial objects without interference from atmospheric absorption.

Instrumentation: Ultraviolet telescopes are often equipped with sophisticated instrumentation, including spectrographs and imaging detectors. Spectrographs analyze the UV light from celestial objects to determine their chemical composition, temperature, and other physical properties. Imaging detectors capture UV images of celestial objects, allowing astronomers to study their structure and morphology.

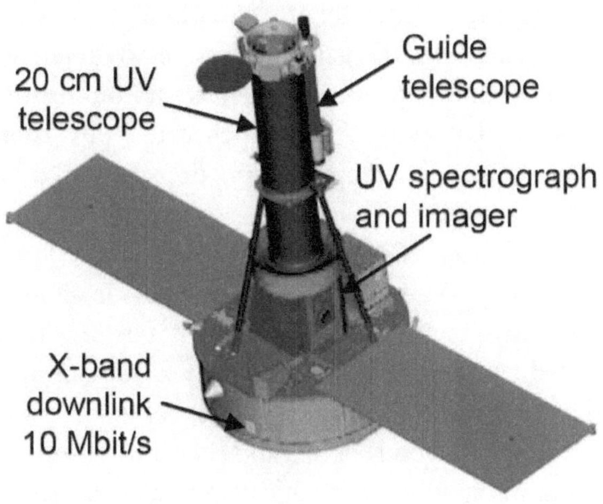

UV Telescope

Studying Hot Stars: Ultraviolet telescopes are essential for studying hot, young stars, which emit a significant amount of UV radiation. By observing these stars in the UV range, astronomers can investigate their temperature, composition, and evolutionary stage.

Probing Active Galactic Nuclei (AGN): Active galaxies, such as quasars and Seyfert galaxies, often emit intense UV radiation from their central regions. Ultraviolet telescopes can study these UV emissions to understand the processes powering AGN, including accretion onto supermassive black holes.

Exploring Stellar Evolution:

Ultraviolet observations help astronomers trace the evolution of stars, from their formation in stellar nurseries to their eventual death as supernovae or white dwarfs. UV light provides valuable insights into the physical processes occurring in stars at different stages of their evolution.

Investigating Interstellar Medium (ISM): The interstellar medium, the gas and dust between stars, emits UV radiation due to processes such as photoionization and fluorescence. Ultraviolet telescopes can study these UV emissions to probe the composition, density, and dynamics of the ISM.

Understanding Galaxy Formation and Evolution: Ultraviolet observations of galaxies provide clues about their formation and evolution over cosmic time. By studying the UV properties of galaxies, astronomers can investigate star formation rates, chemical enrichment, and the interplay between galaxies and their environments.

In summary, ultraviolet telescopes play a crucial role in modern astronomy by enabling the study of celestial objects and phenomena that emit UV radiation. These telescopes provide unique insights into the properties and processes occurring in the universe, advancing our understanding of stellar evolution, galaxy formation, and the nature of the cosmos.

Several space missions have been dedicated to ultraviolet (UV) astronomy, employing specialized telescopes and instruments to observe the universe in the UV portion of the electromagnetic spectrum. These missions have provided invaluable data and insights into various astrophysical phenomena. Here are some notable missions in ultraviolet telescope:

International Ultraviolet Explorer (IUE):

Operational: 1978–1996

The IUE was the first space mission dedicated to UV astronomy. It was a joint project between NASA, ESA, and the UK's Science and Technology Facilities Council. The IUE observed over 104,000 astronomical targets, including stars, galaxies, and quasars, providing important data on their UV emissions and properties.

Hubble Space Telescope (HST):

Operational: Since 1990

While primarily known for its visible and near-infrared observations, the Hubble Space Telescope also has instruments capable of observing in the UV range. The Wide Field Camera 3 (WFC3) and the Cosmic Origins Spectrograph (COS) are two of Hubble's instruments that can capture UV light, enabling studies of phenomena such as star formation, stellar evolution, and galaxy dynamics.

Galaxy Evolution Explorer (GALEX):

Operational: 2003–2013

GALEX was a NASA space telescope dedicated to surveying the sky in the ultraviolet. It studied the history of star formation in galaxies and the evolution of galaxies over cosmic time. GALEX provided crucial data on the UV emissions from young stars, hot stars, and active galactic nuclei.

AstroSat (Ultraviolet Imaging Telescope):

Operational: Since 2015

AstroSat is India's first dedicated multi-wavelength space observatory. It includes the Ultraviolet Imaging Telescope (UVIT), which observes in both near-ultraviolet and far-ultraviolet wavelengths. UVIT has been used to study a wide range of astrophysical phenomena, including stellar populations, active galaxies, and supernova remnants.

Far Ultraviolet Spectroscopic Explorer (FUSE):

Operational: 1999–2007

FUSE was a NASA mission designed to explore the universe in the far-ultraviolet portion of the spectrum. It provided high-resolution spectroscopy of astronomical targets, allowing astronomers to study the composition, temperature, and dynamics of interstellar and intergalactic gas.

Orbiting Astronomical Observatory (OAO) series:
Operational: 1966–1981

The OAO series of satellites included several missions equipped with UV telescopes and spectrographs. These missions provided some of the earliest UV observations of stars, galaxies, and other celestial objects, paving the way for future UV astronomy missions.

These missions, along with others, have significantly advanced our understanding of the universe in the ultraviolet wavelength range, providing crucial data on the properties, evolution, and dynamics of celestial objects and phenomena.

MUON TELESCOPE

CHAPTER EIGHT

MUON TELESCOPE

Muon telescopes are instruments designed to detect muons, which are subatomic particles similar to electrons but heavier. Muons are created naturally in the upper atmosphere when cosmic rays, primarily high-energy protons and atomic nuclei from outer space, collide with molecules in the Earth's atmosphere. These collisions generate a cascade of secondary particles, including muons, which shower down to the Earth's surface.

Muons, as cosmic rays that produce them, present non uniform arrival directions and temporal variations at ground level and, along certain observation directions, could forecast the arrival of interplanetary coronal mass ejections (ICMEs) at the Earth, even earlier than neutron monitors.

Muon telescopes typically consist of layers of detectors placed underground or in shielded areas to minimize interference from other particles. When a muon passes through the detectors, it leaves a traceable signal. By analyzing the trajectories and energies of the detected muons, scientists can study various phenomena, including cosmic ray interactions, atmospheric phenomena, and even geological structures.

Cosmic rays are high energy radiation originating in the cosmos, consisting of nucleonic fragments that rain down on the earth from outside the solar system in the form of Extensive Air Shower (EAS). There are several secondaries generated in these showers. The most common fundamental particles to reach the Earth's surface are muons, electrons, neutrinos,and gamma rays. The easiest way to extract information from these particles is by keeping the detector on earth's surface. By requiring coincidence in several detectors, background radiation will automatically be sorted out.

A muon telescope consisting of two polystyrene plastic scintillation detectors . The Secondary flux has been observed by increasing the distance between the detectors, horizontally as well as vertically.

This study has been extended for observing the flux on keeping the detector inside, outside and on the top (4.5 meters) of the laboratory building. Horizontal separation, vertical separation,data inside, outside and at the roof of the laboratory building, are five measurements performedusing Muon Telescope at constant threshold of discriminator. In this process, one detector was kept at the fixed position and the other detector has been moved with respect to the first one.

SEASA (Stockholm Educational Air Shower Array) in Alba Nova Physics Centre in Stockholm,has performed this detector separation study with three detectors and it has been observed that the count rate decreases with the separation between the detectors because the telescope loses the sensitivity to lower energy shower.

Muon telescope ,Ooty,India

The largest muon telescope in the world is located at the Cosmic Ray Laboratory in Ooty, Tamil Nadu, and is part of the GRAPES-3 experiment. With a cross-section of 0.1 x 0.1 m2 and a length of 6 m, each mild steel square tube accounts for approximately 4000 proportional counters. The muon telescope's unparalleled sensitivity is demonstrated by the finding of a brief weakening of the Earth's magnetic shield caused by space weather and the first measurement of a gigavolt potential in thunderstorms.

The GRAPES-3 observatory located in Ooty, India at an altitude of 2200m meter is designed to study the origin, acceleration and propagation of cosmic rays through measurement of extensive air showers, induced by primary cosmic rays or gamma rays entering the Earth's atmosphere in tera to peta electronvolt energies. It also studies solar and thunderstorm phenomena using cosmic ray muons. GRAPES-3 employs an array of plastic scintillator detectors and a large area muon detector based on proportional counters.

Pierre Auger Observatory

The Pierre Auger Observatory in Argentina is home to the biggest muon telescope currently in use. The observatory is mainly equipped with instruments for studying ultra-high-energy cosmic rays, but it also has detectors for muons.

The Pierre Auger Observatory consists of an array of surface detectors stretched over 3,000 square kilometers, paired with fluorescence detectors that examine the light emitted when cosmic rays interact with the atmosphere. Additionally, buried water-Cherenkov detectors help in measuring the muons generated by these cosmic ray interactions.

Muon telescopes help astronomers study cosmic ray fluxes and their effects on the Earth's atmosphere. They also contribute to understanding high-energy astrophysical phenomena, such as gamma-ray bursts and supernova remnants.

Muon telescopes offer a unique perspective on the universe and provide valuable data for scientists across various disciplines. Their ability to detect muons, which can penetrate deeply into matter and travel great distances, makes them powerful tools for exploring both terrestrial and extraterrestrial phenomena.

Glossary

Refracting Telescope:

Objective Lens: The lens at the front of a refracting telescope that gathers and focuses incoming light.

Eyepiece: The lens or group of lenses at the rear of a refracting telescope that magnifies the image formed by the objective lens.

Chromatic Aberration: Dispersion of light into its constituent colors due to differences in refraction, resulting in color fringing in the image.

Apochromatic (APO): A type of refracting telescope that corrects for chromatic aberration, producing high-quality, color-corrected images.

Doublet: A lens system consisting of two elements designed to reduce chromatic aberration in refracting telescopes.

Reflecting Telescope:

Primary Mirror: The large mirror at the bottom of a reflecting telescope that collects and focuses incoming light.

Secondary Mirror: The smaller mirror near the top of a reflecting telescope that reflects light from the primary mirror to the eyepiece or camera.

Newtonian: A type of reflecting telescope with a concave primary mirror and a flat secondary mirror mounted at an angle.

Catadioptric Telescope:

Corrector Plate: A lens at the front of a catadioptric telescope that corrects for optical aberrations and acts as the primary aperture.

Schmidt-Cassegrain Telescope (SCT): A type of catadioptric telescope that uses a combination of lenses and mirrors to fold the optical path, providing a compact design.

Maksutov-Cassegrain Telescope: A type of catadioptric telescope that uses a meniscus-shaped corrector lens instead of a corrector plate.

Other Terms:

Aperture: The diameter of the primary lens or mirror of a telescope, determining its light-gathering ability.

Focal Length: The distance from the primary lens or mirror to the point where the image is formed or brought to focus.

Magnification: The degree to which a telescope enlarges the apparent size of an object, determined by the focal lengths of the telescope and eyepiece.

Mount: The mechanical structure that supports and aligns the telescope, allowing it to be pointed and tracked accurately.

Field of View: The angular extent of the sky or scene visible through a telescope or eyepiece.

Radio Telescope:

An instrument used to detect and study radio waves emitted by celestial objects in the universe.

Antenna: The part of a radio telescope that collects incoming radio waves. It can come in various designs, such as a dish, horn, or array of dipole antennas.

Feed: The component of a radio telescope that captures the incoming radio waves from the antenna and transfers them to the receiver for processing.

Receiver: The electronic device that amplifies, filters, and converts the incoming radio signals from the feed into a form that can be analyzed and recorded.

Frequency: The number of cycles of a radio wave that occur per unit of time, typically measured in hertz (Hz). Radio telescopes often operate at specific frequency bands to study different phenomena.

Resolution: The ability of a radio telescope to distinguish between two closely spaced objects in the sky. Higher resolution allows for more detailed observations.

Sensitivity: The ability of a radio telescope to detect weak radio signals from distant celestial sources. Greater sensitivity enables the detection of fainter objects and phenomena.

Interferometry: A technique used in radio astronomy that combines signals from multiple radio telescopes to achieve higher resolution and sensitivity than is possible with a single telescope alone.

Array: A group of radio telescopes working together as a single instrument to collect and analyze radio waves. Arrays can be composed of telescopes spread over large distances (e.g., Very Long Baseline Interferometry) or clustered closely together (e.g., aperture synthesis arrays).

Synthesis Imaging: A method used in radio astronomy to create high-resolution images of celestial objects by combining data from multiple telescopes in an array.

Pulsar: A rapidly rotating neutron star that emits beams of radio waves, which can be detected and studied using radio telescopes.

Radio Interference: Electromagnetic signals from human-made sources (e.g., cell phones, Wi-Fi, television broadcasts) that can interfere with radio telescope observations. Radio telescopes are often located in remote areas to minimize interference.

Radio Spectrum: The range of frequencies of electromagnetic radiation, including radio waves, microwaves, and other forms of non-visible light. Radio telescopes observe specific bands within the radio spectrum to study different astrophysical phenomena.

Radio Source: Any celestial object that emits radio waves, such as stars, galaxies, pulsars, and nebulae. Radio telescopes detect and analyze these sources to learn about their properties and behavior.

Radio Frequency Interference (RFI): The contamination of radio telescope data by unwanted radio signals originating from terrestrial sources. RFI can degrade the quality of observations and must be mitigated through filtering and signal processing techniques.

X-ray Telescopes:

X-ray Telescope: An instrument designed to detect and study X-rays emitted by celestial objects, such as black holes, neutron stars, and active galactic nuclei.

X-ray Mirror: A mirror coated with a material such as iridium or gold that reflects X-rays onto a detector, typically made of a semiconductor material like silicon or CCDs (Charge-Coupled Devices).

Grazing-Incidence Optics: A design used in X-ray telescopes where X-rays are reflected at a shallow angle to the mirror surface, minimizing absorption and maximizing reflection.

X-ray Diffraction: The scattering of X-rays by atoms in a crystal lattice, used in X-ray telescopes to analyze the structure of materials and celestial objects.

Chandra X-ray Observatory: A space-based X-ray telescope launched by NASA in 1999, providing high-resolution X-ray images of astronomical objects.

Gamma-ray Telescopes:

Gamma-ray Telescope: An instrument designed to detect and study gamma rays, the highest-energy form of electromagnetic radiation, emitted by sources such as supernovae, pulsars, and gamma-ray bursts.

Scintillation Detector: A type of gamma-ray detector that converts incoming gamma rays into flashes of visible light using a scintillating material, such as sodium iodide or cesium iodide.

Compton Scattering: A process in which a gamma ray interacts with an electron, causing it to recoil and the gamma ray to scatter at a different angle, used in gamma-ray telescopes for detection and energy measurement.

Fermi Gamma-ray Space Telescope: A space-based gamma-ray observatory launched by NASA in 2008, studying high-energy phenomena such as pulsars, black holes, and gamma-ray bursts.

Ultraviolet Telescopes:

Ultraviolet Telescope: An instrument designed to detect and study ultraviolet radiation emitted by celestial objects, including hot stars, quasars, and interstellar gas clouds.

UV-Optical Telescope: A telescope that observes both ultraviolet and visible light, often used to study the properties and evolution of galaxies and stellar populations.

Far Ultraviolet (FUV): The region of the ultraviolet spectrum with wavelengths between 100 and 200 nanometers, studied by space-based UV telescopes like the Hubble Space Telescope.

Near Ultraviolet (NUV): The region of the ultraviolet spectrum with wavelengths between 200 and 400 nanometers, observed by ground-based and space-based UV telescopes for studying stars, galaxies, and planetary atmospheres.

Ultraviolet Absorption: The process by which interstellar gas and dust absorb ultraviolet radiation from stars, creating absorption lines in the spectra observed by UV telescopes.

Muon Telescope:

An instrument designed to detect and measure muons, which are subatomic particles similar to electrons but heavier, typically produced by cosmic ray interactions in the Earth's atmosphere.

Cosmic Ray: High-energy particles, primarily protons and atomic nuclei, originating from outer space and colliding with particles in the Earth's atmosphere, producing secondary particles including muons.

Detector Array: A collection of individual detectors arranged in a specific configuration to detect and track muons passing through the telescope.

Scintillator: A material that emits light when charged particles, such as muons, interact with it. Scintillators are commonly used as detectors in muon telescopes.

Photomultiplier Tube (PMT): A highly sensitive detector that converts light into an electrical signal, commonly used to amplify and detect the faint signals produced by scintillators in muon telescopes.

Muon Flux: The rate of muon detection by a muon telescope, typically measured in muons per unit area per unit time.

Cherenkov Radiation: A type of electromagnetic radiation emitted when charged particles, such as muons, travel through a medium at speeds greater than the speed of light in that medium.

Muon Flux Variability: The fluctuation in the number of muons detected by a muon telescope over time, influenced by factors such as atmospheric conditions, solar activity, and geomagnetic effects.

Muon Energy Spectrum: The distribution of muon energies detected by a muon telescope, providing insights into the sources and processes responsible for muon production in the atmosphere.

Resources

Resources

List of websites, online forums, astronomy clubs, and other resources where readers can find more information about telescopes, connect with other enthusiasts, or purchase telescopes and accessories:

Websites for Information and Resources:

NASA's Night Sky Network: A network of amateur astronomy clubs and organizations supported by NASA, providing resources, events, and outreach materials. (https://nightsky.jpl.nasa.gov/)

Sky & Telescope: A leading publication covering astronomy news, observing tips, and equipment reviews. Their website offers articles, guides, and forums for enthusiasts. (https://skyandtelescope.org/)

Astronomy Magazine: Another prominent publication featuring articles, reviews, and resources for amateur astronomers. Their website includes forums and a buyer's guide. (https://astronomy.com/)

Online Forums and Communities:

Cloudy Nights Telescope Reviews: A popular online community for amateur astronomers, featuring forums, reviews, and discussions about telescopes, observing, and astrophotography. (https://www.cloudynights.com/)

Stargazers Lounge: A UK-based astronomy forum with discussions on telescopes, equipment, observing techniques, and astrophotography. (https://stargazerslounge.com/)

Reddit Astronomy: The astronomy community on Reddit offers discussions, questions, and sharing of images and experiences related to telescopes and astronomy. (https://www.reddit.com/r/Astronomy/)

Astronomy Clubs and Organizations:

The Astronomical League: A federation of amateur astronomical societies in the United States, offering resources, programs, and awards for amateur astronomers. (https://www.astroleague.org/)

Royal Astronomical Society of Canada (RASC): Canada's leading organization for amateur astronomers, with local centers across the country offering observing events, meetings, and resources. (https://www.rasc.ca/)

International Dark-Sky Association (IDA): A non-profit organization dedicated to preserving dark skies and reducing light pollution, with resources and advocacy efforts worldwide. (https://www.darksky.org/)

Online Retailers for Telescopes and Accessories:

Orion Telescopes & Binoculars: A leading retailer of telescopes, binoculars, and accessories, offering a wide range of products for beginners to advanced enthusiasts. (https://www.telescope.com/)

Celestron: Another reputable manufacturer and retailer of telescopes and optical equipment, known for their quality products and innovation. (https://www.celestron.com/)

Explore Scientific: A manufacturer of telescopes, eyepieces, and accessories known for their high-quality optics and innovative designs. (https://explorescientific.com/)

About The Author

Outside of his professional career, Kanchana Munirathnam is actively involved in the amateur astronomy community, participating in local star parties, astronomy clubs, and outreach events. She shares his passion for astronomy through public lectures and online forums, inspiring others to explore the wonders of the night sky.

In his free time, Kanchana enjoys astrophotography, capturing breathtaking images of celestial objects and sharing them with fellow enthusiasts.

Kanchana's dual interests in astronomy and IT complement each other, allowing him to pursue his passion for exploration both in the digital realm and under the vast canopy of stars. Her journey as an amateur astronomer and IT professional continues to be guided by curiosity, innovation, and a deep appreciation for the wonders of the cosmos.

The telescope, I think, most especially... will reveal to us, not perhaps the true proportions of the celestial bodies, but certainly not their apparent diameters."
- Galileo Galilei